The Great Hunger

Karen Douglass

Plain View Press
P. O. 42255
Austin, TX 78704

plainviewpress.net
sb@plainviewpress.net
512-441-2452

Copyright Karen Douglass 2009. All rights reserved.
ISBN: 978-0-9819731-6-6
Library of Congress Number: 2009926075

Cover design by Susan Bright
Cover Art: Kaleidoscope – Organic Squash © 2009, Peach Reynolds

Acknowledgements

    I wish to thank Allison Hedge-Coke for her encouragement in starting this book, and my good friend and frequent first reader Helene Swarts for her support.
    Thanks also to the editors of the following publications in which some of these poems first appeared, some in an earlier version: "Cows," "Immigration & Customs Enforcement," "Citizenship Questionnaire": Spring 2008 in *The Café Review*; "The Rich Man Eats a Cracker" in *Green Mountains Review*; "The Great Hunger" in *NUTS, Naropa's Summer Writing Program* publication, 2007; "The End of Innocence" in *Poets in the Park*; "Thirteenth Street Market" in *Rambler*; and "The Last Supper" in *Texas Review*.
    The poem "Pregnant Waitress" will be published in *Margie*, Vol. 8, Autumn, 2009.

Dedicated to the memory of my grandmothers, who fed me.

Flora Elizabeth Hamilton Boyd, 1896-1952
Gertrude Irene Thibodeau Hill Cole, 1885-1968

Contents

Preface	7
The Great Hunger	9
Against Nature	11
Appalachian Sin Eater	12
Block Party	13
Bloodline	14
Cake	15
Call It a Day	16
Cinderella's Back Story	17
Citizenship Questionnaire	18
Chocolate Anger	19
Cocoon	20
Coffee Break	21
Corn Hag	22
Cows	23
Dancing in the Aisles	24
Dear Trout	25
Dream of Well-fed Birds	26
Eggs for Dinner	27
The End of Innocence	28
First Offering	29
The Great Hunger	30
Greetings	31
"Here's Lucy"	32
I Want to Eat	33
IHOP, Mon Amour	35
Immigration & Customs Enforcement	37
Jack-O-Lantern	38
Kill the Messenger	39
The Last Supper	40
Mama	41
Mapping the Universe	42
Mercy Visit, Paris	43
Mud	44
My Father's Eyes	45
The Neon Dragon	46
Origin of the Honeymoon	47
Pity Is a Full-time Job	48
Prairie Dogs	49

Pregnant Waitress	50
Reading Glasses	51
Requiem	52
Reservations Required	53
The Rich Man Eats a Cracker	54
Salsa Invasion	56
Salt	57
Snow White Turns Fifty	58
Solstice	60
Spanish Bullets	61
Street Vendor	62
Sugaring Off	63
Thirteenth Street Market	64
Too Much, Too Little	65
Tropism	66
Value Added	67
Venus on a Locked Ward	68
What's Here	69
Who Wins, Who Loses?	70
Winter Praise	71
Witness	72
Manifesto	73
A Food Time Line	74
Suggested Reading	79
Suggested Web Sites	80

About the Author   81

Preface

Air, water, food—worldwide these most basic needs are threatened. Planting, harvesting, herding, and shopping allow people to eat, not always well, not always wisely. My compatriots, Americans, mostly shop. We buy heavily processed, industrialized, packaged food. We eat fruit, vegetables, grains, dairy products, and meat from the anonymous hands of agribusiness. Local, small farms suffer, and we risk genetically modified food, irradiated food (often labeled "cold pasteurized"), pesticides, E. Coli, and a host of environmental insults. Seventeen per cent of US fossil fuel consumption currently involves producing and transporting food. Damming rivers for irrigation causes vegetation to rot and contribute methane to green-house gases. Cattle burp and produce methane. Increasingly, we eat food that travels over a thousand miles from field to fork. And we get fatter. We are eating ourselves and the earth to death.

The poems in this collection reflect my relationship to and concern for our food supply, as well as the habits and tastes passed to me by my ancestors and by the merchants who often shape our eating habits. In order to extend the meaning of these poems and to enlarge their context, I have added a food time line as well as a list of books and web sites that I find useful. Given the recent increase in news about unsafe, unhealthy foods, we do well to educate ourselves about what we eat and the real cost of feeding at the current trough. The food web is enormous and complex, and time is short.

The Great Hunger

Against Nature

All the world's a dump
and I'm up to my ankles—

crumbs of paper, loaves of it,
pink Styrofoam eternally ours,

a purple neoprene glove everted
like a prolapsed organ never to rot,

that dandelion yellow cup
propped against the briar rose,

spoor of passersby, ghosts
with living dogs, their waste,

that plastic bag in a tree,
angry wind sock, snap, flap, shred,

paint smears, neon smudge,
potted slop art.

I have no acorn patience;
the world should end in green.

Appalachian Sin Eater

The woman cores sour apples,
sweetens and spices the pie,
pinches the crust tight, sealing in
what she cannot bear to say.
Wipes her hands on an apron
threadbare as faith.

She knows to leave
her sinner's pie, hot and fragrant,
on the window sill and walk away.
The smell will bring him.
Like his fathers before him,
he'll take on the sins of the world.
He'll chew this mountain down.

Block Party

Alley clean, closed off—no homeless here.
Leave white guilt on the front porch,
slip out the patio door. We live here
so our eight year old can play outside,
and expect no one to shoot at him for his fair hair.
Do we apologize for clean houses and double
hollyhocks? Do we apologize for the dog?
Dear god, must I be judged for a dog? Yes, yes,
we own a used piano and an exercise bike,
a patio umbrella on wheels. We eat meat.
The dream we have is the dream we live.
The creed once was greed, our race not pure
in thought or word. But get this: I'm porous.
I recycle. My people survived famine,
cattle boats on the North Atlantic, rock farms, and
textile mills. My people left France, Ireland, England, and
Nova Scotia so that I could, on this particular Sunday
in July, eat hot dogs and coleslaw, sip iced lemonade
in the shade. Here's to you Thibodeau, Hill, Boyd,
Hamilton, Ferguson, Savoie. Here's to all you left in
Poitou, Kerry, Lietrim, Tyrone, and Derbyshire.
Thanks again for another good day.

Bloodline

Now the fainting begins in me,
barefooted in the kitchen
making a terrible white sandwich,

pouring milk, wearing
another bleached cotton gown.
My mother faints; I will not
do it, as I would not leave

marriage behind me for her
divorced sake. My bones whiten in
this fair skin. It will not be

her fault if I fall, spill
milk on the rug. Silly
putting a rug in the kitchen.
Mother did, I did.

Once it starts my body refuses me.
My feet slip out of place.
My eyes see the underside of things

Cake

And where, after all, does hunger fit in?
The moon-pie truck rolls ringing
through the streets, "Get your treats here."
Children cry for cake, gulls newly fledged,
foraging for crumbs from the wide vests of CEO's,
from frosted wrappers on the sidewalk,
sticky as our hearts are sticky, wanting
to share the sweets but stupid about it.
The truck rolls on. We lick our fingers,
full up, pretend cake does not matter
to a starving mouth. Let them eat.
Let's think it over at the supper table.
Life needs more puff pastry.

Call It a Day

Bassoon's cucumber sound
a spoonful of low notes
to fatten a day
brisk with laundry,
robust soup in a new pot—
dice, chop, boil, simmer and serve
a promise of clean sheets.
Murmuring over a salad of
fourth-grade spelling bee,
office politics, what the dog
dragged in, chewed, spit out.

Castled against yellow crime tape,
remains in a nearby ditch—
female with boots—call it
Friday Supper. Oh, call it
refuge at the table.
Offer carrot cake if you can,
cold milk, and a good night.

Cinderella's Back Story

Again peelings from boiled potatoes
fall into the sink. This is not
Food Network. No one here
celebrates KP duty.

Not that I was always dutiful—
those young hours between school bus
and supper never long enough
to sweep the kitchen, start
the potatoes and watch
all of American Bandstand.

Time cared not at all
that I wanted to fly away,
land in the TV studio where
Dick Clark would single me out
for the camera. Channel Eight
cast a dancing spell, and I woke
at the stroke of five—
floor gritty, spuds raw—
cranked the burner to hurry
the boil, boiled the pot dry.

A better girl would dance
with broom and saucepan,
keep time with a paring knife.
I never learned to dance.
I learned to peel potatoes.

Citizenship Questionnaire

Do you swear allegiance
to the White House, Army, Navy,
Marines, Coast Guard, local police
and IRS?

How often do you walk in the park?

Name seven trees native to this country.

Will you recycle?

How much food do you need?

Show that you can cross a busy street
without getting killed.

Calculate the cost of milk, bread,
shoes, a newspaper.

Can you help us? Can we help you?

Sing something in your mother tongue.

Are you kind to dogs and children?

Good, come in, stay with us. Maybe
here the guns won't find you and
you will eat something every day.

Chocolate Anger

Melts over her body,
settles at the hips,
makes itself a present

of pudendum and its dread.
Armor is less strong than
this rage against what love
pretends to be. Pay attention.

She is a bigger target now,
but hard to push around.
Looks soft. She's not.

Hunger's everywhere.
If she's fattened, he can't feed.
She makes herself a hiding place
inside that moving ziggurat,

that altar of herself. First,
she loved him best,
when she was still his child.

Cocoon

(for C.A.)

Weaver leaves the loom unstrung;
writer burns her book;
cook turns down the flame;
drum shrinks in the corner.

Grapes wither without her.

She's a sigh, a long exhale,
for now, building, cell by cell
and fingers first, a new self
in scarlet silk and linen,
one long braid of honor down her back.

She'll bake with new yeast,
call welcome to the sun,
who is her child,
the yeast a faithful spouse.

Coffee Break

Tall anonymous cups
   flat white plates
    balm for a mind
      racing to its own defense
rooting in leaf mold, fallen facts
  that don't add up,
    scratching for crumbs,
expecting
a great white stag
  to walk into this coffee house.
    I have one hour to edit my life.

Corn Hag

When you were young
we loved you, Zea Mays,
fell on our knees, prayed for you.
Our Lady of Guadalupe blessed
the food and protected the farmer.
You were delicate as a girl,
golden haired, shy.
I wore your picture on my shirt,
Corn Maiden with your arms full,
combing the tawny silk.

Now the fields scream Corn!
a warning. You fatten us for the kill,
make us sick and corn poor,
insinuate your hold on every mouthful,
torture our cattle, penned in
with corn-sour stomachs,
force fed in a stench of profit.
Racist, you
strangle strangers, uproot and
plow under anyone not of the clan
Field Corn #2, genetic clones, an army
at attention all the way to the horizon.
You make me cry uncle—
Uncle Subsidy, Uncle Monsanto,
Uncle Manure Lagoon. Corn pimps
are everywhere. But listen,
Corn Hag, whore, I vote with my teeth.

Cows

Two long-horn cattle
graze the hillside along Dillon Road,
narrow throwbacks among squat beeves.
These walking gene pools
have their own secret loves—
the finest bed-down, nightly
comedy of shrill coyotes,
the peaks glowing over Boulder Valley.

They do not know that I scan
the hills as I drive, eager
to see the shadow line of their horns,
evidence that all is not lost,
these cousins of ancient aurochs.
Some good will come of saving them,
hope will come. They remember
in their marrow survival in dry times,
dry, do you hear? We too
will be dry and wise as cattle,
or shrivel like road kill, bowled over,
stupid, stunned in full sun.

Dancing in the Aisles

After the war,
they knew what love was.
They left the house in the care
of dogs and cats, drove
to Shop 'n Save. Overhead
the PA system crooned
"Love Me Tender,"
and between the deli and
the eggplant he held out his arms.
She floated. He glided.
They two-stepped around
bright bananas and mangoes
until a voice said,
"No dancing in the aisles."
He bowed. She smiled.
They bought endive and
tomatoes and fresh basil.
They paid cash.

Dear Trout

Teach me to fish.
I'm hungry.
You flash in the sun,
plunge away.
I'm hungry.
I could dive in to you,
let the wise river take us deeper.
Teach me to swim.

Dream of Well-fed Birds

A boy holds out his arm and
a falcon lands, talons light
on tender flesh.
On the hard street
pigeons gang around a man,
land on his shoulders.
He throws down bread.
I fast, sip strained juice,
pretending for twenty-four hours
to be one of the famished thousands.
The boy carries the wild hawk
to a table where it feasts
like an honored guest.
In a frigid open sky
bodies in motion, crows
correct me. I eat and keep warm.
The pigeons woo fate,
accept manna where it falls.

Eggs for Dinner

Woman at the next table
eats with her pink coat on,
walker folded by her chair.

She's mind-dancing,
Al's dead hand on her back,
jacket ripe with sweat and cigarettes.

Her order's always scrambled now;
she bends her white head down.

One of these days I guess
I'll eat with her, silent,
devoted to a plate of eggs.

The End of Innocence

An old comfort, sorting dried beans,
pintos—spotted ponies—falling
through my fingers. Their label
testifies, "Quality guaranteed.

These beans are a natural product."
Till now this search and sift
meant nothing more than supper
sliding through my hands.

Tonight I find seven black rocks
sharp as teeth, proof of the earth,
proof that the one packing beans
in Skokie, Illinois, blinked

while the ponies ran into the bag.
Risk and belief clatter down the bowl
with the brindled beans and
my jaw aches like a broken heart.

First Offering

My first year married
I brought to the feast
a barely-there pumpkin pie,
tendered it to the aunts,
who could, every one, build a pie
rich and thick, pie with attitude.

Seven months pregnant, I was
not much fun in my big brown dress.
Why not scarlet or sky blue? Why not
more eggs in the pie filling?
I didn't know yet that
I'd been called to feed the world,

didn't know the kitchen as shrine
where any offering matters.
Nourish the family. Bring pie
to our table. Sing pumpkin songs.
That first pie, every pie,
is life homemade. Taste it.

The Great Hunger

My first food memory—hot boiled potato
mashed together with one raw egg.
I am three. The shape of potato is the shape of egg.
I put out my hand and Gram gives me white bread
and butter, folded, a pocketbook.

She taught me not to trust red leprechauns,
just green. She never told me about the long braid
of beauty and terror—fields of potato blossoms,
row upon row of pinky-lavender against dark green,
an acre meant to feed ten people,
then the blackspot, blight, crop failure,
ships loaded with grain
sent away from Ireland to feed an Empire.
Emerald handkerchief fields lay fallow,
the people gone, gone, gone,
two million,
crushed into the holds of immigrant ships
crossing the North Atlantic or
rotting in the ditches, no one to cover them.
Danny Boy's in Boston, his face black and blue,
"Hit 'im agin, he's Irish."

She told me her father's story,
how he ran away from Ulster,
him with the hands of a master weaver,
the rage of an Orangeman,
the thirst of his nation. I'm his child
three times removed. It's my job
to remember things I never saw.

The bellies of bureaucrats still swell and
hang over their belts. The Empire feeds corn
to cows and cars. The famine has moved on.

Greetings

You hated my hair pinned up,
but the heat! You had that old dark
loneliness, Cryin' Time, a drawl
of bodies across the tile dance floor.
Do you recall our life in that latitude
at the end of the present tense?

It's such a fishy business still,
this sex thing. I'll walk toward
the Black Wall, to the K's and find you.
Or not. Did you go home? Does your shirt
still shine in the dark?
We were scared crazy and you
counted on the Viet Cong to end it.

I could throw a barbecue for you
and all the men in my life. I imagine
helping them to coleslaw, each one
wondering why he was invited. I see
the memory creep up their faces
as they put it together, why
I've asked them here, fair, dark,
stout, thin, rugged, elegant.
And now, my gentle men, let's dance;
only clocks and calendars get ahead.
All the men I ever loved still live,
the chairs and tables of my soul.

"Here's Lucy"

I wanted Lucille Ball broadcast into space,
blazing red-headed super nova
bumbling along that great conveyor belt,
pie in the face, flour in her hair.

For years I've thought aliens would find us
funny, frantic clowns, with Fred and Ethel
avatars of next-door good will, proof
we can be trusted to share our canned goods.
We don't have to be abducted.
We'll put on the coffee and set out the Oreos.

Turns out,
our signal can't get off the block,
can't even leave the 'hood. We cannot escape
the gravity of our own network.
Space-time walls us in. It's just us. Don't expect
rescue from the stars. Desi's loudest cha-cha
fades to silence just beyond Jupiter.

I Want to Eat

One raw carrot. I drive ten miles
to Vitamin Cottage—not a cottage,
a chain store where no one says
what goes into bulk foods
in their plastic bags. I buy a bunch of carrots
in their plastic bag with its inky label.
Question the bag, the label. Who
put it there? Stock person at minimum wage.

My carrot rode in a semi,
blowing diesel like bad breath,
driver with her laundry list and
an abscessed molar, the truck, a Peterbilt
with more forward gears than I have brains.
My carrot withers while I ponder.
My stomach growls, "Eat the carrot, please."
Not yet. We haven't calculated the miles
from the California farm to Lafayette, CO,
nor figured the trucker's fuel, tire wear,
tolls, union dues, meals on the road.

Maybe she eats carrots, but
none from the load. They are sealed
and accounted for. Oh, oh, accountant
in this drama, too. Back up,
who put my carrot on the truck?
Forklift driver at the warehouse
after someone stoops again and again,
pulls carrots one by one, lopping off
the greens, tossing the root in a crate.
"Eat the carrot!" Not yet, not yet.

continued...

Carrot seed smaller than peppercorns
has to sprout and swell in a huge field
of sweet soil under California skies,
seed poked into the furrow, earth
smoothed by a groaning harrow
after the plow turns at the end of each row
like a line of verse. The driver
of the John Deere pulling the plow
wears headphones, ball cap, a Bud Lite
t-shirt, jeans. He dreams
as he plows about his third child, a boy,
finally, just born. The boy will not
drive a tractor, not if dad has a say.
"Can we eat?" Almost. We have to
buy the seed and fertilizer, study
irrigation—an aquifer gasping its life away—
sign papers at the bank and the co-op.
Every carrot, every time. Every damned time.

IHOP, Mon Amour

I sigh to hear myself
resist cartoon food,
chemical snack cakes
no one labels:
"Miles of subsidized corn,
tons of final ground water,
long-haul gasoline."
Taste the waste. But—
the woman making frosting,
man running the cream-filling pump?
The snack-cake maker
has mouths to feed, a mortgage,
wants cable TV and health care,
bratwurst on the barbecue.

Forgive me then my sins—
eggs from worried hens,
tortured bacon and
who-knows sourdough,
the danger
of plastic jelly all the way
from Omaha. Don't ask
about the water
to grow my coffee,
ten tons per pound,
the 600 gallons to coax
from Bossie a block of cheese.

continued...

If you are what you eat,
I am the Ogallala Aquifer
that grew the wheat toast.
I am the vet tech docking
the tail of a caged, neurotic hog.
I am that hog. I've eaten
for years. Born with teeth.
Came hungry, I'll leave guilty,
and tip the wait staff as I go.

Immigration & Customs Enforcement

S1639   www.ice.gov

Whose idea to chill our borders?
Metal badge—ICE Officer—not real
gold pinned to a dark uniform.
I cannot explain ICE,
never had to run, duck and cover,
to harvest lettuce or grapes,
put on a nanny dress, hide
my face in false papers.
Border crossing is a curse;
dying of poverty is a curse.
Twelve foot fences
make fourteen foot ladders.
ICE—to kill.

Jack-O-Lantern

The nine year old
goes for a hero costume
making the world safe
for small boys,
cuts the face of vengeance
into a pumpkin,
ready to fire it up,
scare what haunts him.

Something lurks on the porch
among the wilting gourds—
wraith, waif—puff of wind surely,
surely not ancestral ghosts
begging to be heard.

A wolf made into a monster,
a spider or bat not happy
to hold séance with our dead,
vengeful pumpkin maybe,
rotting orange breath,
wasted flesh—as children
beg for packaged sweets.

Kill the Messenger

Dull oasis in orange and neon, this motel
restaurant sheds stuttering sparrows,
leftovers from a dream.

Feeling no mercy for the egg yolks
meant to break like hearts on a plate,
I sop up juices in memory of you.

I left while you were loving all the angles
of a longneck lady. Her father was a Miller
and you love her best, you whose geography

crawls over time zones, leaves messages
from Mexico in Seattle. You packed
your guava-jelly kisses and went south.

Interpol warns the border guards:
"Mexico should lock up its virgins."
Gossip of you reaches home like bonfires

up and down an ancient coast—a siege lifted,
a citadel ruptured. Twice you reappear
with breath like beer and marmalade.

Your pulp-novel life plays tricks and
I cannot out-rage cantina music and
the hiss of rented women. You grow

heated and contagious when I send word,
"Come here. I want you." Breathing hard,
I flag down every bus, ask it to let you off.

Friends dismount lugging a spare tire,
wearing fishing lures in their ears.
Everyone is famished. You are delicious.

The Last Supper

With other women I went early to the well.
We shared the news and the smell of spring.
They had their families and I had paying guests.
We lifted up the dripping jars. Upstairs
I put the bread to rest at the open window.

I picked over the lentils,
letting stones slip like hard memories
through the sieve of my fingers.
The air filled with dust and heat.
The Passover lamb was ready.

Visitors broke bread and ate meat,
talking in deep, strange voices.
They were not from Jerusalem,
with their rough clothes, country manners.
I watched the day die and thought

how glad my late husband would have been
the young rabbi had asked me to cook for him.
And I worried how little oil I had left
and how few olives. It's a long wait
till this spring's harvest. One man left early,

as if he'd had enough. The others went downstairs,
I swept, ran my hands over the benches,
and tossed out the stale wash water
to bless the herb garden. The rabbi's eyes
reminded me of my sister's oldest boy,

lost years ago. At times like that I cry
because I spend my days caring
for other women's sons. I ate the broken bread
and drank the leftover wine. No one said
it was the last of anything.

Mama

The children yank the string
that moves my lips—See mama talk!
Mama is a sideshow freak. She cries
on demand. Our one and only!

My girl sharpens me to a point,
whittles off slivers with her tongue.
I am stuck in the spaces
between her teeth. My second son

throws a nightmare across the floor.
It looks like a chair with claws.
He kicks the wall. It kicks back.
I grow big and dark as a closet.

I am in labor again. Locked out,
the children break in to use me
for a salt lick. They help themselves,
wearing me hollow with their small mouths.

Mapping the Universe

Like an explorer, a salt shaker
has wandered to the coffee table.
I think of traveling too, but

a house full of crumbs ties me down.
The cats leave food on their place mat—
a blue map of lands they will never see.
They eat their kibble and ignore Russia,

old mother country of Nabokov where
the manor house fed the world.
I dream of a map in the dark sky,

lines of light on pure black,
leading me star by star,
to a new order in the sky,
a feast bigger than Russia.

Mercy Visit, Paris

Tell us about the Seine.
Tell us about the book stalls
on the Left Bank, Shakespeare & Co.
You must have seen the Louvre
and the Musee D'Orsay.
Tell about the cheese shops,
the yellow cheddars, ripe and tangy.

How did they slice them? And
the fish, the salt smell and
pearl shine, flash of the knife.
No postcard ever came. Tell us
about the lush vegetables,
the baguettes and croissants,
the new red wines. Your friend,

she left the hospital after surgery?
Were the nurses kind? Were you?
Now tell us again
about the long flight home and
how customs took away
those tangerines. Did it rain?

Mud

I eat fresh cherries, melon, apples.
While I sleep, mind blank as blue linen,
my body squeezes out juices and molecules
and pushes the pulp down the long pipe
of gut, continuous with the tubes and
basins of the sewer.

A moldy orange, arrogance of rot
takes over, ripening in glory. I fling it,
along with bad packaging and coffee grounds,
into the charred dumpster with no lid.
Discreet workers move the orange
to the landfill, where seeds find
neither sun nor true soil, where
ashes of a week's living settle,
compacted by rain, where heavy engines,
filthy, hard running, grind back and forth,
psychotic with grief. They hate their work.

At the stable a man comes in hope of manure;
golden green glory of a summer's grazing
went in as purple clover, sweet feed, oats.
The manure man plans to roll out
miles of custom dirt for roses, peonies, ageratum,
for orchards that burst into psalms of pink-white
dusted loose in a shaking wind. Roots pull up rain
cell by cell, fill the swelling apple, pear,
blood orange. Horses gather to drink,
to wash down timothy hay, to scratch, swat,
stomp bugs that take their blood. Grit, mold,
mud, life ripening in the crannies.

My Father's Eyes

He hands over his coat,
his wallet, his shirt—
Left Eye, Left Eye, mark
his surgical gown left eye,
the chart left eye,
my heart's left eye.

They lead him away
to an inner room;
the surgeon goes
into the cave of his eye
and out, leaves a lens
that works.

An hour passes. In a diner
we order hope over-easy
with bacon, coffee, toast.
He eats like a gangster,
a don in dark glasses—
the one who calls
all the cops "Son."

Four hours later that eye
floats open on its own,
wash of light returning.

The Neon Dragon

This restaurant has to do with desire
for hearth and heaven, belly and soul.
Bright cabinets with glass fronts
hold a geode big as a spaniel,
two glass dragons twined in cellophane,
a statue of Kuan Yin in a gilded robe.
Goddess of Mercy, she glitters and winks.
On the wall a bas relief of Earthly Blessings,
ten children tug a cart of gold coins,
Real fish swim near the register for luck.

I plan to hide under a booth at closing time,
spend the night among the dragons.
Kuan Yin nods. I sit in a perfect lotus, bathed in neon,
listening to the bubble of the fish tank,
hiss of the pilot light, growl of the fridge.
Daylight comes too soon, treacherous
as garlic sauce. I bow to Kuan Yin,
bow to the amethyst geode, bow
to the glass fish and the real fish.
I'm full now.

Origin of the Honeymoon

Like sixty-thousand gold daystars,
bees from four wooden hives huddled
near the edge of the blueberry field
dart nectar to nectar, pollen to pollen,
making the bushes fruit, grasses pregnant
for cows to graze and make rich milk.

Wooden frames hold sheets of wax where
iron-willed females fan the larvae.
In this rigor of production, a whirring
furnace of desire, drones husband the queen.
Then their sisters throw them out to die,
drag them, piece by piece if they have to,
leaving the bodies on the threshold.

If the queen lays good eggs, she lives,
or
the keeper orders a new mail-order bride,
kills the old queen with thumb and finger.
Bees swarming over his face and arms,
the beekeeper cuts open the honey pockets.
One gallon of honey and five of water
will yield an ancient drink thicker than wine—
wildflower mead, meant to make newlyweds fertile.

Pity Is a Full-time Job

Along the bridge rail
a hundred small birds
huddle against the cold,
daubs of shadow
the shape of ripe figs.

What if I harvest them all,
warming and feeding them
around the clock?

One hundred more mouths
chirping day and night,
all atwitter about life and time.

Beaks open and close—
More gruel! More gruel!
And I cancel the rest of life
to grind their endless corn.

Prairie Dogs

Fat, brown busybodies
snacking on sunshine—
I'd be one,
hovering at the burrow,
gossiping. Maybe
I was once,
munching prairie grass.

And what ate me,
coyote, crow, beetle?
I was once lunch,
will be again,
molecule by molecule
spreading into the next form.

I'll feed on sunlight
as we always do,
mind nibbling on dawn
over the lake, loving
a clatter of geese, ducks,
red-wing blackbirds,
feast for the senses
in a candy land of houses,
cars, yellow roses, yellow wasps.

Pregnant Waitress

With no press corps or motorcade
she carries the flag, unfurling it as she walks,
now the rain has stopped.

She carries the flag far from the battlefield
and restores it to its place outside
Uncle Andy's Coffee Shop on Cottage Road.

While she waits for her daughter's birth,
she goes on pouring coffee, making change.
I wish our troops would come home and
protect her.

Reading Glasses

Narrow, so I can look over them
at this banana, and ignore the fine print—
Product of Far Away—pretend I don't know
about gas for long haul trucks, their tires
that can explode, just tear off my head
and these glasses become forensic evidence.

These glasses lie down, arms open, waiting,
a mail-order bride, unsure of what's ahead,
the housemaid biding her time,
keeping her secrets, showing all the world
I'm blind, my lenses too weak to start a fire.

Requiem

Another stone opens its mouth,
ready to tell its story
in whatever language stones use:

A woman gave birth to stones,
swaddled each one in flannel,
offered them gruel of milk and maize,

which they spat out. She hoped
for better children as the stones grew.
Her back broke. They cried and left her

where she fell. They had no hands.
They went hungry and turned over,
put their faces to the ground

when she begged for help.
They piled themselves up
and made mountains. Their mother
lay beside them and became a river.

Reservations Required

New management installed tables and chairs.
No one looked up.

A yellow ceiling sponged blood red
looks like a crime scene, like something
flew high and bled into the plaster,
beating its wings on the molding,
crying in squeaks and squeals,
lunging, flinging itself in a frenzy,
never learning the truth about escape.

I cannot eat under these stains.

At home I eat with the news on,
chew hearty bread in the face of calamity,
soup and salad dusted with mayhem,
one more slice of reality, raw or cooked.
I dine on disaster, murder, assault,
shootings, bombs, car chases, famine,
international treachery and roast beef.
War is my flambé.

The Rich Man Eats a Cracker

Expensive promises bought him
this cruise on Muscongus Bay, his wife
beside him in a matching shirt, neat white hair.
Rocking under them, the ocean lends
suppleness to bodies stiff with patience.
Harbor and gray seals, rare birds sport at the end
of field glasses. The view is invisible
to the landlocked, narrow eyes of another man,

sitting cross legged, ragged, and tossed
in a ditch in town, having lost his footing
when the world pitched and rolled
beneath him: his woman's gone, been gone
a long time coming. If he sits still, body folded
in supplication, she'll come back to raise him
from this bed of ashes and old cellophane,
deliver him from the aluminum cans gathering

like neighbors, their pigeon voices hallooing to him.
The rich man watches his wife watch
the birds, notes how lately she breaks when
he touches her. He offers her lunch.
She smiles, declining. Her death's a wing beat
from the horizon. She lifts the binoculars
to see. The man in the ditch aches to lean
on the boulder at his back, but believes

if he touched it, the rock would crumble
the way dry bread crumbles in his mouth. Also
in the mouth of the artist running amok
on Summer Island, beyond hailing and beyond
sight of the rich man's boat. The man in the ditch
folds his hands into the hollow of his lap
for safekeeping. The painter's hands grip
a pint of deep regret for the copper sunset

which reminds him of ambition. He's eaten
wild strawberries which remind him of
women. Cursed the native roses, which
remind him of women. All things have

symbolized; he runs over neutral spaces,
into the arms of willows, hides in their hair.
The rich man sips beer against the cracker
parching his tongue to salt sadness.
Another day from his wife's days tossed
into the sea. This cruise is too short and
bite by bite, the sun, against his advice,
feeds itself to the horizon.

Salsa Invasion

If I eat your salsa, praise your salsa,
you'll ask me back again,
serve me more salsa, a cycle
of obsequious eating, pompous cooking.

Make do, make salsa—
campaign slogan for the tomato-onion cabal.
Salsa oozes, slops, garnishes, dribbles.
Salsa is a cover-up for stale, bland ideas.
Salsa crawls onto burgers and into old salads,
sounds the opening salvo for any party.

Food is the vote we get
right after air and water.
I'd rather eat a peach.

Salt

You are away, eating
blood oranges in odd rooms,
talking, talking, syllables
like coarse salt.

Days and days,
a rosary of absence,
I eat Cortlands with sharp cheddar.
Not all flesh is exotic.
Come here, take
salt from my hand—
a baited field—
while I beg for
one more taste of you,
one more bite of the apple.
All flesh is not equal.

Snow White Turns Fifty

She's fingered the old sugar tongs
in her apron pocket all morning.
That day The Prince kissed the apple

from her mouth, he promised her
a fairy tale. Seventeen years
she sat at the far end of the banquet.

Bells clapped, peasants fed her fame.
She tried to stay with him.
Waving from the balcony, she stiffened

her spine to balance a gaudy crown.
She tried instituting economic reform, but
the maids waited, strewed gold

in her path, raisins, and bird-of-paradise
feathers, women possessed by a good idea.
Until one day

she pitched most of a sterling tea set
down the front steps. A beggar passing
caught the pot on one bounce and

stuffed it into his sack — fenced the whole
find, except the sugar tongs still
in her fist; he bought a condo at the beach.

Snow peered in the mirror, began to see why
her stepmother had a hobby, so
she packed, tucked the tongs in her bosom

and lit out on the next coach
heading back to the woods, where
Dopey opened the door — he did

for every passing ninny, despite
his growing up near witches, and there
they were, The Seven, startled at

their beer and cards and jazz on the Sony.
They waltzed her in with a flourish,
herb tea and honey, Oreos and Snickers,

and Snow knew from Sneezy's yellow face
they lived on saturated fats and needed
Cheerios. After hugs she gave in

to palace gossip: how The Prince had
spun his old man into an early grave, and
which duchess dallied with what count. Bashful

blocked both ears, and Grumpy allowed
he'd guessed as much. Then Snow cleared
the cups, aired her old room, announced

she wanted her job back, upon which
Doc cursed the slowdown at the mine, but
offered her minimum wage and full medical.

Now it's another birthday, and if she knows
her boys, they have cake in their pockets.
But she aches and fidgets, fears an early fall.

She wonders if The Prince ever put a new roof
on the East Wing. It's just that memory matters
after all. That's all. Happy Birthday, Doll.

Solstice

Belief sits like meat on the table before us.
I fix the roast, mash the potatoes.
The old world has shriveled to a candle flame
in the middle of the table.

Why don't we fall to our knees, given
the huge labor that delivers light to us,
as we begin the long slide
down the apex of planet and sun?

A new-born sun rises on Stonehenge, shining
on the round dance and the feast of candles.
Green trees march out of the forest
to stand vigil in the corner, jeweled dowagers.

Solstice is coming, coming, coming.
The sun gong ascends. Psalms and
drums and flutes and songs bring us
from the long dark to the blessing of light.

Spanish Bullets

Half moon, one star
take memory hostage—
corned beef and beer
at Pedro O'Hara's,
stories of Spanish Civil War—
bullets blew up, fell short,
plugged the barrel,
refused to kill the enemy.

I took the night as my hostage,
freeze framed, still do.
Memory's grip on your arm
chokes out the months between,
wants every time we meet to talk
about those bullets, badly made, impotent,
to chew that sandwich,
sip from the endless pitcher.

Memory fires with more range.
Aim high. Higher.
Draw a bead and
blow the image out of the water,
shoot it with a camera.
Break it down, reassemble.
Not done yet. Never done
feeding desire.

Street Vendor

Day in, day out, I push
a creaky vegetable cart
through rutty streets,
harking like Molly Malone
my wares. I am not selling fish,
silvery and symbolic, and
exotic fruit defies me. Kiwi
and casabas go sullen, pulpy,
avocadoes practice kitchen warfare
in their leathery green uniforms.

Even apples sulk and pucker.
I've studied like love charms
sexy poems about eggplant,
not platonic vegetables.
I must quickly stew up parmigiana
and Imam Ibaldi or they break my heart.
Potatoes resist me. False hearted
and grimy, they peer from their hovel,
then sprout like devils in the mind.

Bad actors. Weeds I can grow.
Today half a pound of kudzu,
tomorrow—tomorrow
grief grows like a tree, but
today I'll make something
from this vegetable life.

Sugaring Off

Uncle Abe hung a swing
in the sugar maple nearest the house,
sanded the seat, painted it blue.
I learned to fly on that swing,
learned to think under that tree.

He made me a red dress
to see how the sewing machine worked,
built a hutch and stained it
with cordovan shoe polish
because he could. Never
owned a new car, new house,
never had money in the bank.

He drilled a spigot into each maple,
early spring, warm days, cold nights.
Lugged forty quarts of sap to make
one quart of syrup, hours
stoking the wood fire
up hill from the house. Snow
still patching the empty pasture.

He set that hot jar of syrup to cool
in the snow. It burst.
He started over. His son died
at a year. Two girls came.
He never let them out of his sight,
lest they break.

Thirteenth Street Market

Dirt, sweat, sandals, ponytails,
dogs in red bandanas—I love
Boulder's Farm Market.
I buy goat cheese and tomatoes,
admire Asian lilies, golden beets,
baby bok choy, purple basil,
beans, corn, asparagus, onions, garlic.

I'm shopping for salvation here,
putting money in my mouth,
betting on green to save us.
Pushing back against a brick tide,
against big-box economy and
corner-store ease. I am learning
to live one squash at a time.

Too Much, Too Little

On Bataan Uncle George
dressed his cup of rice
with motor oil
strained through bread.
He lived to show me
fiddleheads and pink teaberries
hidden in the underbrush.
My teeth crushed
their sweetness in my mouth.
He said I need never go hungry.

I am hungry.

My apple heart has no core,
no center pentangle of seeds.
I never make it to the bone,
to the corn-tassel ripeness.
A clutch of grapes plunges
over the white edge of a bowl.
Mushrooms wait for the knife,
the cast iron pan, the olive oil.
Parsley, basil, oregano—
these words remind me that others
are starving. At the window
a breeze hums over the mouth of a jug,
kid with a pop bottle, native flute.
I am not alone. The world does not
have enough food to go around.

Tropism

The biology of love is not
the rough rake of the harvest

a weighted cry of joy
or weltered grief of absence

but the warm heaviness
and mess of life—

blind leaves turned sunward
no more thinking than

an infant at the breast
open mouthed in hunger and in awe.

Value Added

Coins slide through my fingers, change
into blueberry bagels, Columbian coffee,
cream and butter.
                    Money
clogs my arteries, coats my tongue,
rots my teeth.
                    Dollar bills
like dry leaves blow away,
pennies embed themselves in tar,
dimes and quarters stick in the gears.
                    Money
makes me a wife to my job—
chides the footloose
to make their bed while worry nibbles
on hours and days and years
till life's an empty box of bonbons,
its breath the rustle of small papers
and the rasp of a cardboard cover.
                    Gold
coats the many roads to hell.
It ties my hands to the tiller
through the hurricane.
It buys my ticket home.

Venus on a Locked Ward

Weird girl, you disturb us.
Your organic madness comes
from a time before Harlow or Gable

or Madonna and those women
who take asylum in magazines,
wearing cherry-berry lip gloss. You

push apple cores into body cavities.
You wear wilting gardenias to dazzle
your bare breasts. We murmur, cover them.

The container is the thing contained.
In the first world you would call us
to a remarkable wedding feast

where your people bow down
to the oranges laid at the altar
of your baby's picture.

We worry about this child;
the fruit you offer has
a stab wound in its navel.

What's Here

An iron pot, too heavy to put away,
sits in the dark and the daylight,
certain of its future, cold stove or hot,
full of soup or the hope of soup.

Other women envy that pot,
notice it, pat its black belly.
In summer it sits thirsty,
all mouth without words,
handles built in, lid well met.
Nothing escapes.

Come winter, I oil it up,
set it on the front burner,
dump in what's here.
No two soups ever the same.
Who deserves such a pot?
Just luck, chance,
but I'm hanging on.

Who Wins, Who Loses?

First the simmering pot, clothes dryer,
buzz and rumble of machines—
behind the wall, they go about
their business while I
listen over a book, sensing
if any jar or jug or mug
wanders
shelf to shelf. I wake
just knowing the soap
has walked into the flour,
salt married sugar,
and the man I love
has burst through the hall
and escaped through
the refrigerator door,
walked into that light
between the vanilla yogurt
and the mayonnaise.

Winter Praise

Winter's bride has been veiled
from our eyes. What begins
as breeze becomes a gale.

She comes as an eared owl,
an eagle, outwitting me.
Her eyes are brown and bright.

Her plan is to reside on the road
and squat down, give birth
to a green apple with a brown stem.

Witness

The horse crunches grain,
   noses the feed dish around

so he can see the horizon line,
   his job to watch what's coming.

I lean on his warm bay shoulder.
   I am in charge of the sky,

the dusk fading, cold west light,
   rising half moon, and

a long, long ribbon of geese
   flowing south on the solstice.

We are part of a live tableau
   that does not fall apart,

the geese a hundred souls
   drawing the edge of winter over us.

Manifesto

- I will not knowingly support hunger, greed, disease, animal cruelty, and slave labor in the service of food production.

- I will support local, concerned farmers who provide food free of artificial hormones, antibiotics, pesticides, GMO's, and other contaminants.

- I will curtail other spending in order to pay fairly for what I eat.

- I will support government policies and proponents leading to a clean, affordable, regional food supply.

- I will vote with my teeth.

A Food Time Line

18,000 BC: Bow and arrow come along; hunters still use pits to kill herds of animals too big to wrestle to the ground; Horses are hunted to extinction in America and will have to wait to return on board Spanish ships.

7000 BC: Potatoes grow in central Peru.

2475 BC: Maize, potatoes, and sweet potatoes on the menu in Western hemisphere.

1493: Christopher Columbus brings pigs to America.

1497-99: Long ocean voyages to the new world lead to scurvy among the crews. Vasco da Gama loses 100 men.

1500's: 150 varieties of potato are under cultivation in Peru.

1570: Potatoes are finally raised in Europe, meant to feed hospital inmates cheaply. This will eventually affect the US, which does not yet exist.

1644: Coffee comes to France. The US will be so glad, once it is born.

1780: Potatoes grow in Ireland, meant to feed ten people to the acre. Stay tuned, importance still TBA.

1842: Dear, darling, John Lawes produces the first chemical fertilizer. Oh, shit!

1845-49: In the Irish Famine one million die and one million emigrate, many to the US. Ships loaded with Irish grain leave at the behest of Great Britain. Thanks so much for the help. See Swift's "A Modest Proposal."

1847: Chocolate bars are marketed by the Fry family in York, England. These folks are Quakers interested in combating the ingestion of alcohol. The US will have to wait for Mr. Hershey.

1864: Margarine is invented, using beef fat, skimmed milk, and cows' udders.

1865: Along with the American Civil War (how uncivil), here comes the explosive harpoon for killing whales.

1870's: James Salisbury promotes meat extract and invents the ground meat patty. (Special sauce, lettuce, pickle and onion on a sesame seed bun all come later. In fact, we have over 5000 burger joints in the world.) Thomas Lipton opens a chain of stores in the UK, but now we just have his tea. Refrigerated rail cars come into use; now we need food that lasts a long, long time, no matter what it takes to make it last. Bring on the nitrates.

1874: Alfred Parker, the Rocky Mountain cannibal likes the taste of miners.

1875: Luther Burbank opens a market garden business, develops the Burbank potato, which leads to the Idaho russet. Bing cherries, yum, are discovered on a tree in the Willamette Valley, a chance seedling nourished by a gardener named Bing. Nothing to do with Chandler from the sitcom *Friends*.

1888: Drought in North America raises fears of Global Warming. US for the first time imports grain for its domestic needs.

1889-90: Droughts continue in American Midwest. Drought in India and China kills about 60 million people. Corn flake crusade begins as J. H. Kellogg encourages folks to eat cereal.

continued...

1900: US has a population of 75 million; 6 million farms; that's one farm for every 12.5 people.

1906: Upton Sinclair's The Jungle exposes the dirty secrets of meat packing. Pure Food and Drug Act passes, requiring labels that list the contents of packaged food.

1909: Enter the electric toaster in US; also peppermint Life Savers and Quaker Puffed Wheat. Ed McCollum first isolates Vitamin A.

1916: President Wilson signs the Federal Farm Loan Act.

1927: Borden starts homogenizing milk.

1929: 7UP comes on the market.

1931: Huge US wheat crop causes price collapse and a lot of pissed-off farmers. By the end of the year, breadlines form throughout the country. This year sees the first television broadcasts, which lead us straight to the Food Network and virtual food as virtual entertainment.

1932: In US 30% of workers are unemployed; "Buddy, can you spare a dime?" This is also the birthday of Fritos and Skippy peanut butter.

1933: Hungry peasants in Spain are arrested for gathering acorns. Probably the squirrels filed a complaint, asked for a restraining order. Nutty, huh? In the US it's hello to Ritz crackers.

1934: Dust storms affect 150,000 square miles of Middle America. Okies take to the road. "California or bust!"

1940's: Slogan in the US is "Vitamins will win the war." We threw A bombs at Japan, and all we really needed was A, B12, C, D, E, and K

1961: I graduate from Potter Academy and Rachel Carson publishes *Silent Spring*.

1962: US ships 88 million pounds of powdered milk to Brazil, but no one in Brazil likes powdered milk.

1964: US starts issuing food stamps.

1967: US sends 20% of its wheat crop to India.

1975: Pop Rocks explode onto the market.

1976: The average American eats 68 pounds of beef in a year.

1983: McNuggets hit the market.

1989: Alar (daninozide) sprayed on apples and ingested, is found to be carcinogenic, but is not pulled by the gov. Growers voluntarily stop using it. This chemical from Uniroyal continues to be sold abroad.

1990: Maine produces 28 million pounds of lobster, a new record. And the 20 millionth can of Campbell's tomato soup goes out the door.

1991: Cops find that Mr. Jeffrey Dahmer has a fridge full of human body parts. Borden—those homogenizers—build a $50,000,000 pasta factory with a yearly production of 250 million pounds. Millions starve in Sudan, Angola, Mozambique, and Somalia; Hershey Foods pays $180,000,000 for 18% of a candy company in Oslo.

1992: USDA introduces the food pyramid to replace the long cherished four basic food groups. We still got fatter. Pyramid schemes don't work.

continued...

1993: More than 10% of Americans rely on food stamps. Calgena, Inc. uses DNA technology to produce GMO tomato called Flavr Savr, said to resist spoiling. And Monsanto markets BST, a genetically engineered hormone meant to increase milk production. So overproduction drives down milk prices and forces small farms out of business. Meanwhile, at the strip malls everywhere, Wendy's opens 330 new outlets for a total of 4200 worldwide.

1994: Thousands of Rwandans die of hunger and related diseases; in the US 4.9 million American elders are hungry or malnourished because they cannot afford to eat well. Some of those who can afford food are too ill to shop and cook. The number of US farmers is lowest since 1850; only 1.9 million this year.

2000: The six billionth human being is born, somewhere. What will we feed this child?

Suggested Reading

Berry, Wendell. "Manifesto: The Mad Farmer's Liberation Front," a poem, at www.goodnaturepublishing.com/poem/htm.

Fernandez-Armesto, Felipe. *Near a Thousand Tables: A History of Food*, The Free Press, 2002.

Jackson, Wes. *Becoming Native to this Place*, Counterpoint Press, 1996.

Kingsolver, Barbara. *Animal, Vegetable, Miracle*, Harper Collins Publishers, 2007.

Lappe, Frances Moore and Anna Lappe. *Hope's Edge: The Next Diet for a Small Planet*, Tarcher, 2002.

Pearce, Fred. *When the Rivers Run Dry: Water, the Defining Crisis of the Twenty-first Century*, Beacon Press, 2006.

Planck, Nina. *Real Food: What to Eat and Why*, Bloomsbury Press, 2006.

Pollan, Michael. *The Omnivore's Dilemma*, Penguin, 2006.

Pollan, Michael. *In Defense of Food*, Penguin, 2008.

Schlosser, Eric. *Fast Food Nation*, Houghton Mifflin, 2001.

Smith, Alisa and J. B. Mackinnon. *Plenty: One Man, One Woman, and a Raucous Year of Eating Locally*, Harmony Books, 2007.

Suggested Web Sites

Context Institute: www.context.org
Extraordinary Books for a Healthy Planet: www.100Fires.com
Food Routes: www.foodroutes.org
The Land Institute: www.landinstitute.org
Slow Food International: www.slowfood.com
Small Planet Institute: www.smallplanetinstitute.org

About the Author

Karen Douglass currently lives in Colorado. Her previous books include *Red Goddess Poems*; *Bones in the Chimney* (short fiction and poetry); *Green Rider, Thinking Horse* (non-fiction); and *Sostenuto*, (prose poems). *Lost Rose*, a novel, is seeking publication. She holds an MA from Georgia Southern and an MFA from Vermont College. For nearly two decades she has been a member of the editorial staff for *The Café Review*, a poetry and art quarterly. You may visit her at kdsbookblog.blogspot.com.

www.ingramcontent.com/pod-product-compliance
Lightning Source LLC
Chambersburg PA
CBHW071839290426
44109CB00017B/1870